Frogs

By Julie Guidone

Reading Consultant: Susan Nations, M.Ed.,
author/literacy coach/consultant in literacy development

WEEKLY READER®
PUBLISHING

Please visit our web site at **www.garethstevens.com**.
For a free catalog describing our list of high-quality books,
call 1-800-542-2595 (USA) or 1-800-387-3178 (Canada).
Our fax: 1-877-542-2596

Library of Congress Cataloging-in-Publication Data

Guidone, Julie.
    Frogs / by Julie Guidone.
        p. cm. — (Animals that live in the rain forest)
    Includes bibliographical references and index.
    ISBN-10: 1-4339-0025-4   ISBN-13: 978-1-4339-0025-9 (lib. bdg.)
    ISBN-10: 1-4339-0107-2   ISBN-13: 978-1-4339-0107-2 (softcover)
    1. Frogs—Juvenile literature. 2. Rain forest animals—Juvenile literature. I. Title.
  QL668.E2G855   2009
  597.8 9—dc22   2008036332

This edition first published in 2009 by
Weekly Reader® Books
An Imprint of Gareth Stevens Publishing
1 Reader's Digest Road
Pleasantville, NY 10570-7000 USA

Copyright © 2009 by Gareth Stevens, Inc.

Executive Managing Editor: Lisa M. Herrington
Senior Editor: Barbara Bakowski
Creative Director: Lisa Donovan
Designers: Michelle Castro, Alexandria Davis
Photo Researcher: Diane Laska-Swanke
Publisher: Keith Garton

Photo Credits: Cover © RF/Masterfile; pp. 1, 17 © Phil Savoie/naturepl.com; p. 5 © Piotr Naskrecki/
Minden Pictures; p. 7 © Michael Durham/Minden Pictures; p. 9 © Heidi & Hans-Jurgen Koch/Minden
Pictures; pp. 11, 21 © Mark Moffett/Minden Pictures; p. 13 © Gail Shumway/Getty Images; p. 15 ©
Christian Ziegler/Minden Pictures; p. 19 (large) © Michael & Patricia Fogden/Minden Pictures; p. 19
(inset) © Petra Wegner/Alamy

Printed in the United States of America

1 2 3 4 5 6 7 8 9 10 09 08

Table of Contents

Boldface words appear in the glossary.

Wet World

More than 2,000 kinds of
frogs live in the **rain forest**.
Rain forests are warm,
wet woodlands.

A frog's skin must stay **moist**. The wet rain forest is a good place for frogs to live. Did you know that frogs breathe through their skin? They get water through their skin, too.

Glass frogs live in the rain forest. A glass frog's skin is almost see-through. You can watch the frog's heart beat by looking at its belly!

glass frog

A High Home

The red-eyed tree frog begins life in water and then takes to the trees! The tops of most trees make up the **canopy**. The canopy is like a roof on the rain forest!

red-eyed tree frog

The red-eyed tree frog is **nocturnal** (nahk-TER-nuhl). It leaps from branch to branch at night. Special toe pads help it cling to leaves and vines.

toe pads

During the day, the tree frog rests under leaves. Its green body blends in and hides the frog from **predators**. Predators are animals that kill and eat other animals.

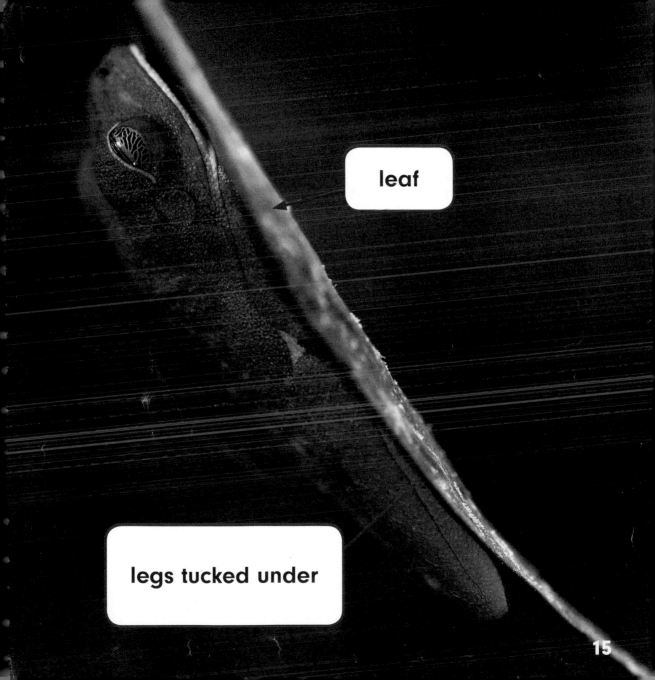

leaf

legs tucked under

15

When predators are near, the frog opens its big red eyes. The bright color scares away animals in search of a meal.

eyes

Colorful Warnings

Poison dart frogs live in the rain forest, too. Their brightly colored bodies are the size of your thumb!

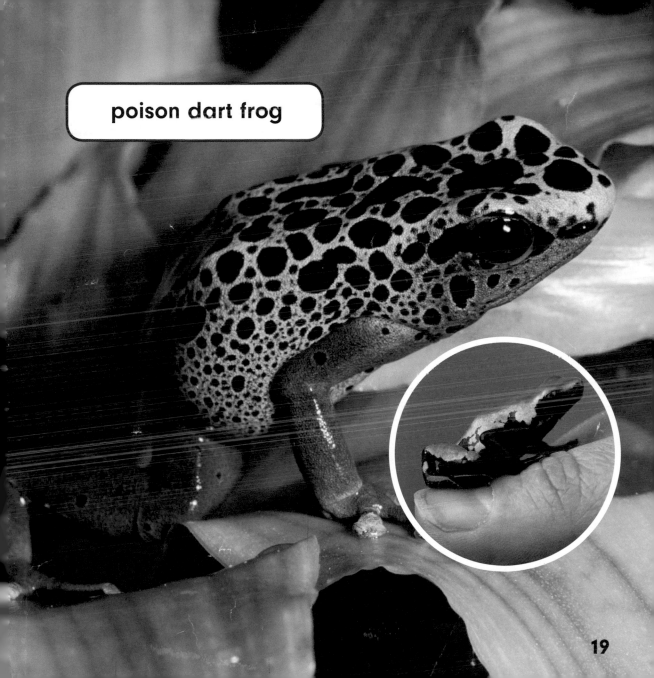

poison dart frog

Bright colors warn predators that the frog's skin has poison. Animals that eat the frogs get sick. Predators learn to stay away from poison dart frogs!

spider

Glossary

canopy: the top layer of a rain forest

moist: partly wet

nocturnal: active mostly at night

predators: animals that kill and eat other animals

rain forest: a warm, rainy woodland with many types of plants and animals

For More Information

Books

Rain, Rain, Rain Forest. Brenda Z. Guiberson (Henry Holt and Co., 2004)

Red-Eyed Tree Frogs. Early Bird Nature Books (series). John Netherton (Lerner Publications, 2001)

Web Sites

Rain Forest Frogs at Animal Corner

www.animalcorner.co.uk/rainforests/paf_about.html
Find facts and photos of poison dart frogs.

Red-Eyed Tree Frogs at Enchanted Learning

*www.enchantedlearning.com/subjects/amphibians/
label/redeyedtreefrog*
Label and color a picture of a red-eyed tree frog.

Index

About the Author

Julie Guidone has taught kindergarten and first and second grades in Madison, Connecticut, and Fayetteville, New York. She loves to take her students on field trips to the zoo to learn about all kinds of animals! She lives in Syracuse, New York, with her husband, Chris, and her son, Anthony.